THE ONLY BOOK A KID NEEDS TO READ ABOUT CORONAVIRUS EVER

BY DISGUSTING DOCTORS

Disclaimer

www.disgustingdoctors.com

ISBN Paperback: 978-1-8382171-0-5

10 9 8 7 6 5 4 3 2 1

Editor Adria Carey
Cover Design by: Mickey Chan
Illustrations by: Ana Villaranda
Interior Design by: Rachael Ritchey

"You have to write the book that wants to be written. And if the book is too difficult for grown-ups then write it for children."

Madeleine L'Engle
Author, New York

TABLE OF CONTENTS

SECTION 3: Stopping the Speedy Spready of Coronavirus

SECTION 4: The Race to Find a Cure

Don't miss the sneak peek of
More from Disgusting Doctors
at the end!

INTRODUCTION

A mind-boggling number of discoveries and inventions have been made over the last century! Around one hundred years ago medicine was revolutionized by Doctor Alexander Fleming. Like most doctors, Dr Fleming is a Disgusting Doctor. We call him this because of his avid fascination with all gross things, bacteria and fungi alike, which led to the discovery of the world's first antibiotic, penicillin. To this day, it remains the most common antibiotic used around the world.

Since then humans have continued to make huge strides. The internet has evolved over the last few decades, changing the face of the world. It is difficult to imagine life without it. Humans reached new heights with the first moon landing in 1969, achieving the impossible. Even flying across the globe has become as normal as, well, flying across the globe!

So why then, with all this grand innovation, have we not been able to deal with a tiny virus?

In 2019, the coronavirus started to spread. It moved from continent to continent, wreaking havoc along the way. The world came to a halt. The disruption took everyone by surprise. Leaders looked to doctors and scientists to solve the problem. Scientists worked around the clock to gather information about the virus. Doctors helped by poking and prodding patients, gathering disgusting bodily fluids to be tested.

Knowledge from previous pandemics and new facts have been presented to leaders. Despite this, they continue to squabble over how best to deal with it. It is not just the virus that is spreading, many myths are spreading too! Some people think that wearing a mask makes you sicker. Others believe that coronavirus was created by an evil scientist in a lab! This has led to widespread confusion.

This book is written by Disgusting Doctors to explain what the coronavirus means for you. Inside, you'll find lots of funny cartoons to help explain the complicated facts that most people don't understand.

Let's begin the journey to separate fact from fiction. You will uncover:

- Why a crab's blue blood is a key ingredient for a coronavirus vaccine.

- How dabbing can save your life.

- How to crush coronavirus with just a phone, pen and a piece of paper.

- The link between coronavirus and skateboards.

- Why Alpacas are important in treating the coronavirus.

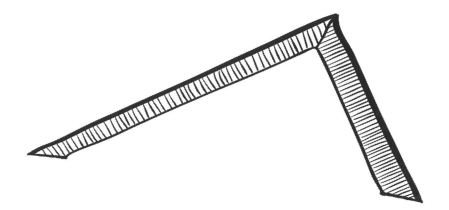

SECTION 1:

All About the Cunning Coronavirus

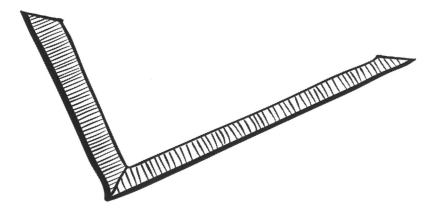

Cunning Coronaviruses

Yes, you read that right. Coronaviruses, plural, not singular! There are lots of things people don't know about coronaviruses. For starters, there is more than one type. The frightful fact is that there are seven types that can infect humans. Did you know coronaviruses aren't even new? The first human coronaviruses were discovered all the way back in the 1960s. The coronavirus that you've heard of is actually part of what scientists call a "family" of viruses.

FOR THE LAST TIME! STOP ANNOYING YOUR SISTER!

Coronaviruses have been known to be infecting unsuspecting humans for around 60 years. However, they are likely to have been roaming the Earth for much longer. An insane amount of time longer! Coronaviruses are thought to have been around for a whopping 55 million years or more. They have mostly been infecting animals in that time. Unfortunately, from time to time, doctors discover a new coronavirus that can infect humans.

The Novel Coronavirus

In 2019, doctors discovered a new coronavirus in China. They didn't have a name for it, so they called it the Novel coronavirus. Novel means new in Latin. (Doctors often use Latin words to make them sound smarter than they are!)

Scientists eventually decided that they couldn't call it "new" coronavirus forever, so it was given its own name: SARS-CoV-2*.

*From this point SARS-CoV-2 will be referred to as coronavirus. Let's face it, SARS-CoV-2 is not the catchiest of names!

Why Are Doctors so Disgusting?

There was a time when not much was known about the human body. Doctors of the past relied on guesswork and sometimes even trial and error. They were naturally disgustingly curious and wanted to understand the human body better. Some disgusting doctors resorted to cutting up rotting corpses, often stolen from a local cemetery! Their thirst for knowledge didn't stop there. Many doctors spent years studying foul bodily fluids like poop and saliva. They collected these "precious" samples and sent them carefully to the laboratories. There, other doctors and scientists marveled at the viruses under electron microscopes. By studying the different samples, they were able to learn more about viruses and how they affect your insides. Their disgusting, inquisitive nature has really paid off with countless discoveries that have been made!

Did you Know?

Doctors use a chart to help determine the type of poop you have. Maybe you can use this handy chart the next time a Disgusting Doctor asks about your bowel motions.

BRISTOL STOOL CHART

	TYPE 1	Little bunny droppings	SEVERE CONSTIPATION
	TYPE 2	Sausage shaped, lumpy and hard	MILD CONSTIPATION
	TYPE 3	Sausage shaped, but with cracks	NORMAL
	TYPE 4	smooth soft long like a snake	NORMAL
	TYPE 5	Soft and in little blobs	LACKING FIBRE
	TYPE 6	Mushy and fluffy	MILD DIARRHEA
	TYPE 7	Completely liquid, no solid bits at all	SEVERE DIARRHEA

BONUS POINTS: SEE IF YOU CAN FIND ANY SWEET CORN!

Where on Earth Did the Coronavirus Come From?

We still don't know. Scientists around the world are yet to agree on the answer. However, despite all the quarrelling, it is widely believed to have come from wild animals.

Shopping Spree at the Wet Market

A wet market is an outdoor market where you can buy fruit, vegetables and meat. Many markets also sell live animals. Before you start thinking it's like a big outdoor pet shop, it's not. Most of the animals sold there are for cooking and eating, like chickens or ducks. These markets are very popular throughout Asia. Most people treat them like supermarkets and go there for their grocery shopping. Occasionally, more exotic animals are sold there, too.

The coronavirus was first reported in a city called Wuhan in China. Nearly everyone who became unwell had been in the same wet market. Some people worked there and others had been there for their daily shop. Many scientists believe the virus could have come from one of the animals being sold there.

Bat Diaries

Most coronaviruses that can infect humans come from one particularly grubby animal, the bat. Bats live in caves and these are the perfect wet, mucky, dingy environments that viruses love to grow in. The good news is that most bats have little interaction with humans. The bad news is that they do interact with some animals that humans eat or use for medicine.

Nobody quite knows which animal actually infected the first human. Many scientists think it could be a mammal called the pangolin (which looks like a scaly anteater). Some people in parts of Asia eat them as a delicacy. Many people also value them for their use in Chinese medicine. In fact, they have been hunted so much they have become an endangered species!

PANGOLINS

SCALES

It has now become illegal to sell wild pangolins. Great news because they are so cute!

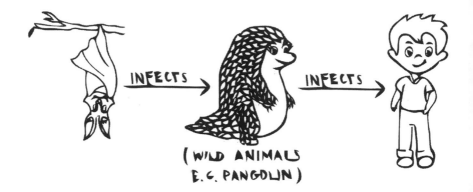

INFECTS → INFECTS →

(WILD ANIMALS
E.G. PANGOLIN)

The Link Between Coronavirus and Skateboards!

Most new coronaviruses that can infect humans seem to come from wild animals. So, the closer humans live to wild animals, the more likely they are to catch potentially deadly viruses from them.

You might be thinking, "Well that's great. I don't live next to any wild animals."

That's a good start! However, what if you knew the wood from a skateboard or the toilet paper you use to wipe your bum could lead to more viruses appearing!

How?

Every year forests are chopped down for wood and paper. This is the natural habitat for many different species of wild animals. Clearing forests destroys their homes! They are left with nowhere to live and end up moving closer to humans. This makes it easier for viruses to spread from wild animals to humans.

Was the Coronavirus Made by an Evil Scientist?

Nobody knows for sure where the coronavirus came from. Most scientists think that it came from wild animals. Naturally, a few people disagree and have their own theories. A theory is just a fancy word for an idea about why something may have happened. You might have a theory about who ate the last donut at home (hint: it was probably your dad!).

One theory is that coronavirus was made in a laboratory by evil scientists and released on purpose to cause havoc! It is true that sometimes scientists grow viruses to test treatments and come up with vaccines. However, this is always with viruses they already know about and not new viruses.

There is (so far) no evidence for this theory, and it's far more likely it came from nature and not an evil scientist!

The Devious Virus

The coronavirus is a typical virus in many ways. Like most other viruses, it can infect humans without them being aware. Viruses are sneaky little things. You can't see them with the naked eye. Doctors find them disgustingly interesting and spend hours examining them under an electron microscope. Once a person becomes infected, the virus can cause major disruption to the cells of the body making them feel unwell.

DID YOU KNOW:

The human body is made of trillions of cells. The cells are like lots of little Lego blocks stuck together to make a human. We have different types of cells for different parts of our body. For example, our noses are made up of cells, guts are made of cells, even our bums are made of cells! Depending on where it is, these cells have different functions. For example, the cells in your nose help you to smell, the cells in your gut help move food along and you guessed it, the cells in your bum help you to poop!

CELLS OF THE BODY

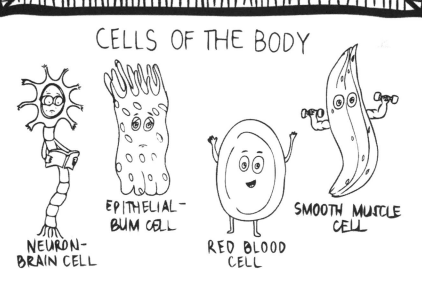

NEURON-
BRAIN CELL

EPITHELIAL-
BUM CELL

RED BLOOD
CELL

SMOOTH MUSCLE
CELL

EXTRA FACTS FOR BRAINIACS

There are two types of microscopes that scientists use to see really small things. Light microscopes have been around for hundreds of years. They are excellent for seeing things like bacteria. However, viruses are much smaller and cannot be seen using a regular light microscope.

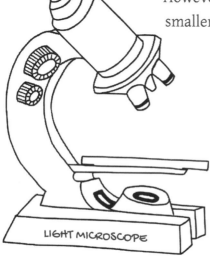

LIGHT MICROSCOPE

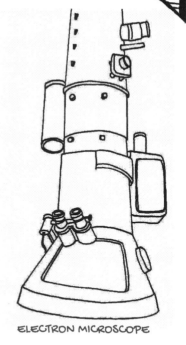

ELECTRON MICROSCOPE

The electron microscope was invented in 1931. They work by shooting a small ray of particles called electrons to get images of minuscule things like viruses. They are able to magnify things up to 1 million times the size. This is compared to light microscopes that can magnify things up to 1 thousand times.

You wouldn't believe how many viruses there are on Earth. Well, there is a whopping quadrillion quadrillion!

How many zeros does a
quadrillion have?
1 000 000 000 000 000
000 000 000 000 000

Don't panic, only about 200, that we know about, can infect humans!

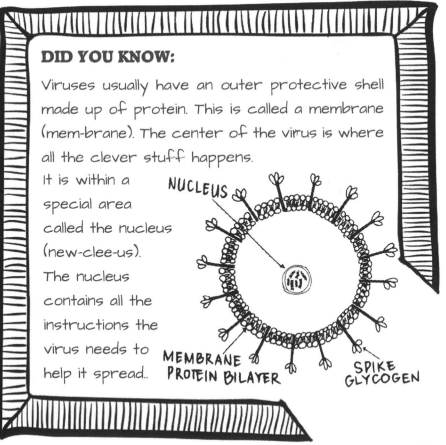

DID YOU KNOW:

Viruses usually have an outer protective shell made up of protein. This is called a membrane (mem-brane). The center of the virus is where all the clever stuff happens.

It is within a special area called the nucleus (new-clee-us). The nucleus contains all the instructions the virus needs to help it spread.

NUCLEUS

MEMBRANE
PROTEIN BILAYER

SPIKE
GLYCOGEN

The Virus that Wears a Crown

The coronavirus is shaped like a soccer ball with spikes. Scientists thought the spikes looked like a crown, so they named it coronavirus. Corona means crown in Latin.

The coronavirus uses these spikes to attach to human cells and infect them. Once inside, they seize control! They do this by combining their genetic code with the cell's. It is sort of like hacking into a computer.

Once it has hacked the cell, the virus is free to replicate (make more copies of itself). With the new copies, it can spread easily to other cells of the body and wreak havoc!

EXTRA FACTS FOR BRAINIACS

Is a virus alive?

You could be forgiven for thinking the answer is yes. After all, viruses do replicate, kind of like animals have babies.

But the short answer is NO.

Viruses cannot replicate by themselves. The only way for them to survive is to infect an animal or a human. The virus uses the energy and materials from these animal or human cells to make more copies of itself. Therefore, scientists have classified them as NOT a living organism.

The long answer is more complicated than that and becomes philosophical. What does it really mean to be alive? We won't open this can of worms right now!

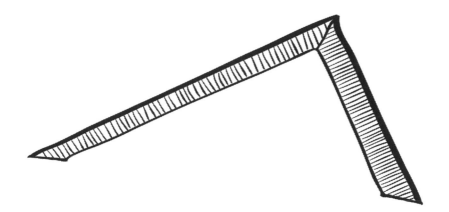

SECTION 2:

Pesky Problems Caused by the Coronavirus

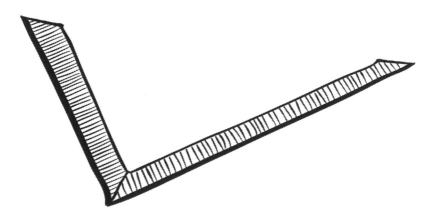

The Virus Invasion

Coronavirus's favorite places to enter the human body are through mouths and snotty noses. Once a person is infected, the virus spreads to different parts of the body. People can begin to feel unwell after a few days, and for others it can take two weeks.

The illness usually starts with an annoying cough, followed by feeling hot and sweaty. Doctors call this high body temperature a fever. These problems, like cough and fever, are called symptoms (simp-tums). Doctors like to use big words to look clever! However, once you know what they mean it is all actually very easy!

There are many other symptoms of the coronavirus apart from cough and fever. When the virus attacks your nose cells, it can reduce or sometimes even stop your sense of smell. Of course doctors have another fancy name for this. They call it anosmia (anoz-meeya). Coronavirus can also reduce your sense of taste. This could come in handy for those awful school lunches!

Because coronavirus is so new, discoveries about how it affects your body are still being made. Scientists now think that a very itchy rash can also appear as one of the first signs of coronavirus. For some people this rash will be on their hands and feet and looks similar to an allergic reaction, sometimes called hives.

EXTRA FACTS FOR BRAINIACS

Did you know the human body has a built-in thermostat in the brain? A special section in the brain called the hypothalamus helps your body temperature stay constant. Viruses also have a perfect temperature that they like. It happens to be the same temperature as the human body! During a fever, the body temperature goes up. This makes it more difficult for the virus to survive. So although feeling hot and sweaty feels awful, fevers are not all bad! They are your body's way of fighting infection.

WHAT DO YOU CALL A SICK DOG?

A HOTDOG

SYMPTOMS OF CORONAVIRUS

COUGH
FEVER
CHILLS
LOSS of SMELL
DIFFICULTY BREATHING
ITCHY RASH
SORE THROAT
RUNNY NOSE
TIREDNESS
VOMITING
DIARRHEA

The virus can just about affect any part of the body, which leads to lots of different symptoms. Not everybody has every symptom!

Sadly, in a small number of people, coronavirus can make it difficult for them to breathe. This means they sometimes need to go into hospital to get oxygen and other treatments.

Fear not, it's not all doom and gloom! The majority of people that get coronavirus don't get very ill. They may only have a slight cough and sometimes fever without any other problems, and they make a full recovery very quickly.

The illness caused by coronavirus is called Covid-19.

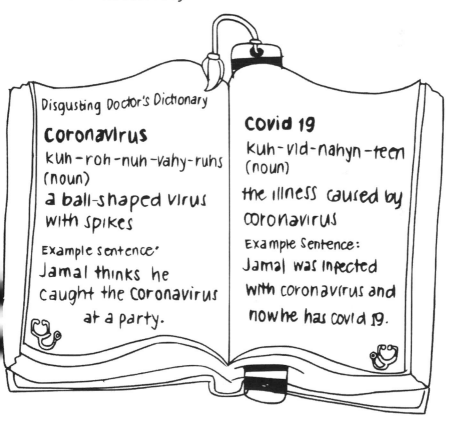

Disgusting Doctor's Dictionary

Coronavirus
kuh-roh-nuh-vahy-ruhs
(noun)
a ball-shaped virus with spikes

Example sentence:
Jamal thinks he caught the coronavirus at a party.

Covid 19
kuh-vid-nahyn-teen
(noun)
the illness caused by coronavirus

Example sentence:
Jamal was infected with coronavirus and now he has covid 19.

But I Feel Fine!

Surprisingly, there are a huge number of people that have been infected with coronavirus that have NO symptoms! That's right, none at all! Often, they don't even realize they have been infected. In fact, most kids will have no symptoms. Of course you will know by now that doctors have a super long unpronounceable word for this. They call a person with no symptoms asymptomatic (eh-simp-tom-at-ic). Pay careful attention to this as it looks just like symptomatic, but with an "a" in front and means the opposite!

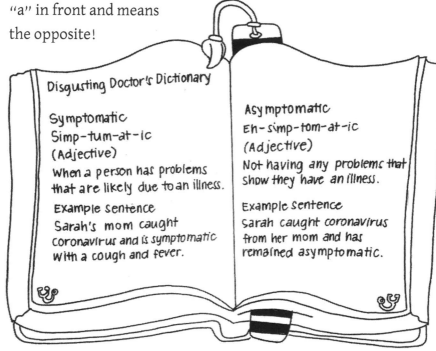

Disgusting Doctor's Dictionary

Symptomatic
Simp-tum-at-ic
(Adjective)
When a person has problems that are likely due to an illness.

Example sentence
Sarah's mom caught coronavirus and is symptomatic with a cough and fever.

Asymptomatic
Eh-simp-tom-at-ic
(Adjective)
Not having any problems that show they have an illness.

Example sentence
Sarah caught coronavirus from her mom and has remained asymptomatic.

For some reason, even though the virus has gone into their cells, it doesn't seem to affect the way the cells work. They do not get any cough, fever or anything in fact. This is disgustingly confusing! Don't worry, even doctors don't know why this is.

Oblivious Spreaders

It sounds like good news that most people don't have any symptoms at all. After all, what could be the problem if they are infected but not unwell? Unfortunately, the problem is that these asymptomatic people can still help spread the virus. In fact, you could argue they are more likely to spread the virus. This is because they do not know they are infected and carry on meeting others as normal. We will explore this a little later.

THESE 5 PEOPELE ARE ASYMPTOMATIC. THEY ALL FEEL WELL.

THESE 3 PEOPLE HAVE MILD SYMPTOMS, THEY FEEL UNWELL, BUT DON'T NEED TO GO TO THE HOSPITAL

THESE 2 PEOPLE HAVE SEVERE SYMPTOMS. THEY NEED TO BE IN THE HOSPITAL.

Coronavirus in the Classroom

Think back to the last time someone in your classroom had a cold (a runny nose or cough). You may have noticed lots of other kids became unwell soon after. Even the teacher may have taken a sick day. Sucks for them, but great for you!

So how did the coronavirus spread from one person to the other?

It's very straightforward, actually. When someone with a virus is coughing, sneezing and spluttering all over the place, tiny little droplets of snot and spit come shooting out.

So revolting when you think about it! These droplets are often too small for you to see and are full of the virus. Even if you do manage to dodge the snotty downpour, you're still not in the clear. The droplets can land on your desk or chair and can stay there for hours or even days! If you touch either of these surfaces you could pick up the invisible virus on your hands. If you then touch your face or scratch your nose it can infect you. (Remember we talked about how these troublesome viruses love to get into your cells through your nose and mouth!)

The obvious solution is not to touch your face. However, it's not as easy as you think. People touch their faces constantly. It's a strange thing humans do for no reason at all. Why don't you try this out on your teacher? Count the number of times they touch their face over the next hour. The average number of times a person touches their face is an astonishing 24 times an hour!

A virus can spread by way of almost anything. The culprit could be a desk, pencil, eraser, sharpener, book, chair, scissors, glue stick, fidget spinner or iPhone, anything really.

DID YOU KNOW:

Did you know humans shed their skin?

Yes, just like snakes! Humans shed about 500 cells every day, and while that might not seem a lot, let me put it like this: it can add up to 1.5 pounds per year in weight. That's the same weight as 2 boxes of Cheerios!

Dust is a nauseating concoction of dead skin cells and dirt. So be careful the next time you see a dusty bookshelf and don't think anything of it. It could easily be swarming with skin cells!

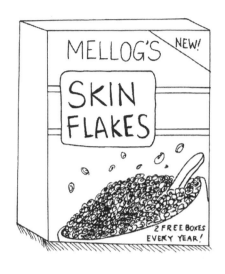

If that wasn't gross enough, this next bit will really turn your stomach. Viruses can be spread by poop. Yes, poop!

If someone goes to the restroom and doesn't wash their hands properly, they could be carrying little poop particles on their fingers and in the crevices of their nails!

If they then prepare a sandwich, the person eating it could become infected. So next time you're in Subway, make sure the sandwich maker has their gloves on (unless you don't mind little bits of poop in your mouth)! Also, it goes without saying, always wash your hands after going to the restroom!

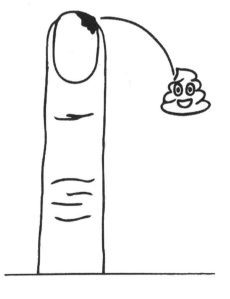

Back to Those Oblivious Spreaders

You know asymptomatic people can spread coronavirus. The question is, how can they spread it if they are not coughing or sneezing?

The answer is in their spit! Literally. They can spread it from their saliva! When talking or singing, especially loudly, little particles of spit can come launching out. Do you know anyone who spits when they talk? Might be worth taking a couple of steps back the next time you're talking to them. You never know what kind of nasty viruses their spit could be carrying!

Pesky Pandemics

Traveling was so common in the 21st century that coronavirus was able to spread throughout the world easily. A disease that affects a large section of the world is called a pandemic. The coronavirus was declared a global pandemic on March 11, 2020, by the World Health Organization. This is not, however, the first pandemic that the planet has had to deal with. There have been many previous pandemics in the past. The deadliest pandemic in human history was the black plague in the 1300s. It is reported that up to 200 million people are thought to have died.

W - world

H - Health

O - Organization

DID YOU KNOW:

The World Health Organization was set up in 1948, sometimes referred to as WHO. It is an international group of doctors and scientists who meet to discuss problems concerning health around the world. Governments often seek advice from them to manage health problems affecting their countries.

Vulnerable Residents

The coronavirus can spread and infect anyone. Different people react differently to the virus. Some people, as you already know, are asymptomatic, and others only have slight symptoms. Unfortunately, there is a small percentage of people who become very sick.

Doctors have worked out ways in which they can keep these people safe and stop them from catching coronavirus. They are described as "vulnerable residents." This means they are more likely to become unwell when they are infected with the virus.

Experts decided the best way to keep them safe was for these vulnerable people to stay indoors until the virus settles down. This is called self-isolating or shielding, and it may have been why you weren't able to see your granny for a really long time (what felt like forever!).

It is not just grannies and grandads that need protection. There are other people that can be vulnerable to viruses, also. The following groups of people are at risk, too:

- **People with severe lung problems (for example, very bad asthma or cystic fibrosis)**

  This book isn't big enough to give you a detailed description of how everything inside the body works, so you should know that lungs are like two big bags of air in your chest which help you breathe. People with lung problems who get coronavirus can have difficulty breathing.

- **People with organ transplants**

Organ transplants are when Disgusting Doctors might take out a slimy kidney from one person and stitch it up inside another person. It doesn't have to be a kidney. It could be other organs (heart, lungs, liver). Don't worry, they don't just do this for fun. Usually the person who gets the organ needs it!

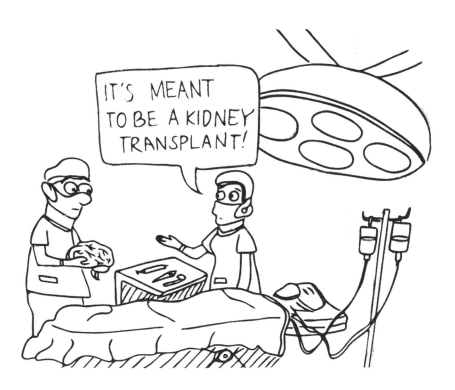

- **People who are getting treatment for cancer**

  Treatment for cancer can be very toxic to the body. It can make you feel sick and weak. It can also make it harder to fight viral infections.

- **People with leukemia, lymphoma, myeloma**

  These are types of blood cancer which make it harder to fight viral infections

- **People with some blood disorders such as sickle cell**

  Remember we told you that your whole body is made up of cells? Well, so is your blood! Sickle cell is a condition in which the cells in your blood are shaped like a crescent moon instead of the normal full moon shape, like in the cartoon here.

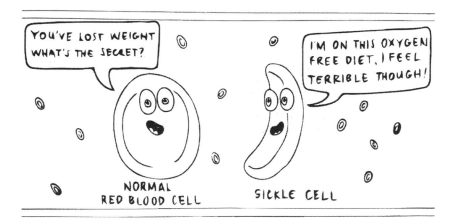

- **Pregnant woman with heart problems**

  Pregnant women with heart problems are more likely to get unwell with coronavirus.

- **People taking immunosuppressant (wow, that's a huge word!) medicines**

  Disgusting Doctors love looking smart! This is just a word for medicines which stop your immune system from fighting infection. Read the vaccines section for more information on your immune system.

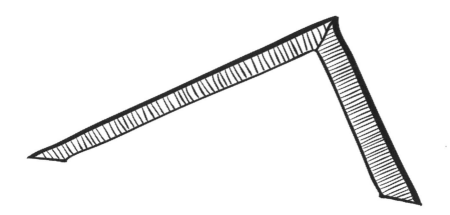

SECTION 3:

Stopping the Speedy Spread of the Coronavirus

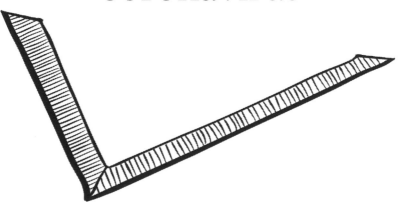

Stopping the Speedy Spread of Coronavirus

Coronavirus spreads from people being in close contact. Diseases that spread like this are sometimes called a contagion (con-tay-jun). Limiting this physical contact can help slow the virus down.

Here are all the steps you need to follow to crush the coronavirus. These range from things you can do to keep safe, and things you can do to keep others safe. You are well on your way to viral expertise!

Social Distancing

One of the simplest, most effective ways to crush the coronavirus (or any virus in fact) is through social distancing. In fact, it has been done for previous pandemics, too!

At the time of the black plague, scientists didn't know what a virus was. People were dying from a mysterious disease and they had no idea why. Some came up with absurd theories about the position of the stars causing the illness! Despite this silly theory, they still managed to discover that keeping a distance from others could stop them from getting sick.

The principles of social distancing are the same as they were hundreds of years ago. Keep a distance of 2 meters (or about 6 steps) between yourself and anyone who doesn't live in the same house as you. Remember this is only relevant to people you don't live with, so you can't use it as an excuse to avoid your brother or sister no matter how annoying they are!

This space between you and other people makes it harder for the virus to spread. A gloopy projectile piece of snot launched unwittingly from a sneeze might miss you and land on the floor if you're not standing too close!

Hand Washing: The Tale of the Humble Soap

This is by no means a riveting tale. However, it might just save your life and others, too, so it's well worth a read.

The coronavirus is the nasty villain in this story. The coronavirus wears a suit of armor to protect itself (it's called a membrane, which we talked about earlier). The one thing we know about baddies is that they all have a weak spot! The coronavirus is no different. The armor is made up of proteins, which are stuck together using lipid as the glue. Lipids are a type of fat (think of it as grease). This is where our unlikely hero comes in, soap. Soap loves to attack fat and grease. The soap annihilates the virus by breaking down this lipid glue and causing the membrane to fall apart. It also makes your hands slippery and the harmless virus parts easily wash off down into the drain. Although it might not seem like it, every time you are washing your hands you are going to war with the virus!

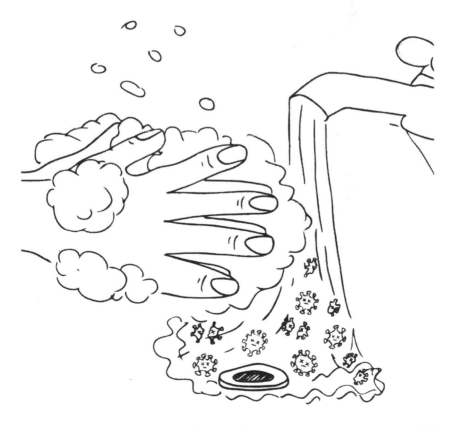

You should wash your hands for at least 20 seconds to make sure the soap has enough time to attack the virus.

It is truly mind-boggling that humble soap, invented thousands of years ago, can be so effective in crushing coronavirus. Handy tip, soap is not just for your hands. You can use it for all your smelly bits!

Hand Sanitizer

When the coronavirus news first broke, people went mad for this gloopy liquid! It is mainly made of very strong alcohol mixed with a gel. The way it attacks the virus is similar to soap, breaking down the weak lipids. Stores everywhere were sold out, and people even started reselling it online for whopping amounts of money! Here's a little secret for you: soap is much better! That's right, once again the humble soap wins.

Hand sanitizer will work, but it is not as good as soap. First, you need to use a lot more of the stuff to effectively destroy all the virus particles. Also, because you are not actually washing your hands the dismembered virus corpses will just stay on your hands (there's a grizzly thought!).

Of course, if you are out and about, you may not have access to a sink or soap, and hand sanitizer is the way to go!

Catch It, Trash It, Kill it!

This next solution for crushing the coronavirus is even simpler than soap. Your mom has probably been telling you to do this forever. Cover your mouth when you cough or sneeze! People don't want to see the insides of your slimy mouth let alone get covered in your gruesome juices! The best thing to do is to use a tissue to catch the snot or spit and throw the used tissue away in the trash.

Dabbing to Save a Life

Don't worry if you need to sneeze but don't have a tissue on you. Use your hands instead and wash them with soap straight after. What if you are out and about, say on a bus, and have no tissue and nowhere to wash your hands? Then you should cough into your elbow. You don't want to cough on your hands and then leave your slithery residue on everything you touch. The added bonus is you can disguise this as a dab. That's how dabbing could save a life!

These simple solutions help crush the
virus and help us keep others safe.

HOW TO COUGH LIKE A BOSS

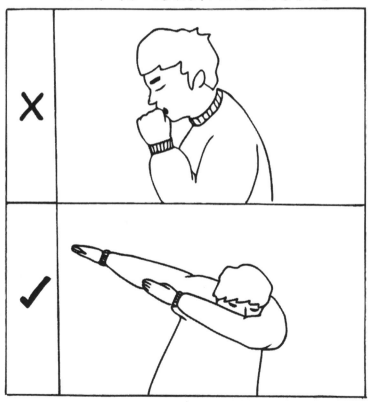

Masks

Masks are cool! There is no doubt about it. All of your favorite superheroes have been wearing them forever. Even the most Disgusting Doctors will use masks to protect themselves against the gruesome fluids that can come gushing out when poking around inside their patients!

Masks act as a barrier between your mouth and nose and the outside world. It is like a wall stopping both your snot and spit droplets from getting out and infecting others. They work best when everyone wears them. This is particularly important when you are in a confined space and can't socially distance from others, such as in a bus or cramped train.

Most masks are good at stopping coronavirus droplets from getting out and infecting other people. This next bit is a little confusing, even for the experts! Masks will not stop all coronavirus droplets from getting in and infecting you! Why are masks good at stopping viruses escaping but not as good at stopping viruses coming in? The reason is complex, and its best explained using peeing toddlers!

FACEMASK EXPLAINED USING PEEING TODDLERS

Imagine: The pee is coronavirus, and the pants are masks.

The two have no pants on. If Ben pees on Jack, Jack will get completely covered in pee.

Jack is wearing pants and Ben pees on him. Only some pee will get through Jack's pants.

Ben and Jack are wearing pants. Now if Ben pees, the pee stays in his pants. Jack stays dry.

Unfortunately, only specialized masks are good at stopping virus droplets from getting in. These masks are usually much harder to get, and often in short supply. They are called filtration masks and stop fluid from getting in. This is why they are usually reserved for essential workers such as carers and drivers. You will hear more about these essential worker heroes in later chapters.

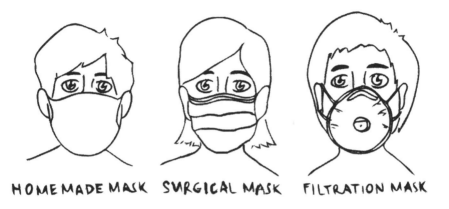

HOMEMADE MASK   SURGICAL MASK   FILTRATION MASK

Masks work much better when more people wear them. If the droplets can't get out of other people's masks, then you don't have to worry about them getting into yours.

Specialized masks are not easy to make and are usually made in factories all around the world. When there aren't enough masks to go around, you can use things like scarves or homemade masks made out of old t-shirts as an alternative. These work pretty well, and you can get really creative with their designs and colors!

HOW TO MAKE A FACE MASK OUT OF AN OLD SHIRT

Please get an adult to help you.

①

Use a ruler to measure out 5-6 inches from the bottom. Carefully cut out a rectangle from the bottom of the shirt.

②

Use a ruler to measure out 6 inches from the side of the rectangular fabric. Leave a strap around half an inch thick top and bottom. Cut this section out carefully using the scissors.

③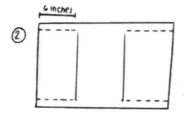

You're almost there, you just need to cut the string fabric, about half way.

④

Put the mask on and tie the fabric top and bottom to secure.

Myths Debunked by Sensible Suliman

Do not, I mean it, DO NOT touch your face!

This sounds like the simplest solution but in practice probably the hardest to follow. You already did the experiment on your teacher to see how many times they touch their face in an hour. How many was it? If you can avoid touching your face, then do it. But you probably can't, so don't worry about it. Confused? So is everyone else. Move on to the next part.

Clean, Clean, Clean

Take a look around you. The terrible truth is that your desk, the pens, the door handle and railings could be swimming in a ghastly soup of human juices. Most of these are, in normal times, harmless, and you don't need to get too worried. However, during a pandemic it's wise to be extra cautious. You can use wipes to clean these surfaces and items. Failing that, you can just use good old-fashioned, yep you guessed it, soap and water! Make sure you don't use water on electronics such as a phone or computer. Don't be that weirdo that tries to wash their phone in the sink!

Gloves

What else can you do, you ask? Well, if you want to be extra cautious when you are out doing your grocery shopping, you could wear disposable gloves. This would stop your grubby fingers covering every apple in the shop with coronavirus! Gloves are probably not needed and better kept for hospital workers as they can sometimes be in short supply. Hey, at least now you know why some people are going around with funny blue gloves on!

Helping Others in Lockdown

The dreaded lockdown. No more school. No more meeting up with your friends. No parties. No school trips. No work. No going to the beach on the next hot day for sunbathing. Life came to a halt.

Most states in the US imposed some sort of lockdown. This means you needed to stay at home and go out only for essential reasons. Essential reasons are things like shopping for food, going to see the doctor if you're sick and collecting medications from the pharmacy.

Unfortunately, this put some people in a difficult position. Many older and vulnerable residents were told to shield. This meant they were not able to leave the house to do their errands.

Those who had family relied on them for help. Others had to turn to neighbors. In some ways, lockdown brought communities closer together. Neighbors who normally didn't speak began checking up on each other. Younger people offered to do shopping for elderly residents in their area. Grandchildren cooked meals for grandparents and left them at their front door.

School's Out for the Spring

Lockdown meant schools were forced to close. Hey, every cloud has a silver lining! Who doesn't love impromptu days off school? However, this elation may not have lasted long. Many children around the world faced the disappointment of canceled school trips and events. Sports tryouts, dance competitions, fundraisers and school proms were all put on hold. The one saving grace was that everyone was in it together.

When Your Mom Is Your Teacher, Your Lunch Lady and Also Your Coach

Did you know even before the pandemic almost 2 million kids in the USA were already being homeschooled? The coronavirus meant that many other kids also had to stay home and be taught by their parents. Some parents let the power get to their heads and even made their kids wear uniforms while at home (that really sucks!).

Working from Home

Work, just like school, could not continue as normal. A lot of workplaces can be tightly packed with people close together. For coronavirus, this would be the perfect place to infect lots of people! To slow the spread, many people were told to stop going out to work. Some were quite fortunate and could easily do their work from home. If your job involves using a phone or computer, you're in luck as this can be done from anywhere! However, not all jobs can be done from home, for example, construction workers and hairdressers.

Social Physical Distancing

Social distancing is a silly phrase, really. Although you are meant to keep a physical distance, you're still allowed to socialize. People need each other. They need daily interaction with their friends and family. Life would be pretty dull without others!

Luckily, you live in the 21st century and there is a lot of great technology at your fingertips to help you stay connected! Many people took to their computers and smartphones to keep in touch with friends and family. Apps like Zoom, Houseparty and FaceTime helped people feel less isolated. Imagine during the black plague, having to write letters to your friends and waiting weeks for a reply!

What's even better than chatting with your friends online? Playing with them virtually in online multiplayer games like Fortnite or Animal Crossing!

Social Media Hysteria

There has been another virus, besides coronavirus, that has been spreading, too. Tik Tok dances have been going viral! Doctors and nurses who have been fighting the virus have been doing dances on social media at work to raise spirits. Social media has helped people keep in touch with friends and family around the world when traveling has been restricted.

Social media has, however, caused problems, too. A lot of false information about the coronavirus has also been shared around. This is often called "fake news." It can be hard to differentiate between facts and myths and this has caused widespread confusion.

Although this example of fake news seems obvious, others are not so easy to spot. It's important to check the source of anything you read online.

Healthy Body, Healthy Mind

What have you been doing to keep active? With all this free time, and with all the gyms being closed, a lot of people have taken up cycling. People have been going for a lot more runs and doing exercise in their gardens and local parks. For those that live in an apartment, exercising at home has really taken off. There are many online fitness classes to keep people motivated. Keeping active is amazing for positivity and general wellbeing!

The Great Toilet Paper Shortage of 2020

When lockdown was announced around the different states, panic started to set in. People began stocking up on essentials for their homes. These included goods like pasta, long-life milk, baking products and, of course, toilet paper!

In March, toilet paper was flying off of the shelves. The sales of it were over seven times greater than at the same time the previous year. Many people bought huge quantities, as they worried about running out during lockdown. By the end of March, **70%** of grocery stores in the US were completely out of stock.

So, some people had huge stacks of toilet paper at home, while others couldn't find any at all, not even online.

The reality is that no one actually needed more toilet paper. The shortage only happened because everyone was panic buying. If people just bought their fair share, there would have never been a shortage in the first place!

Essential Workers

If you have been watching the news, then you will have heard the phrase "essential workers" many times. It is actually very simple! It is a special term that has been given to those people who have important jobs that can't stop during lockdown. For example, everyone that works in a hospital or supermarket is known as an essential worker.

I'M NOT SAYING I'M A BIG DEAL BUT...

WORLD'S CUTEST GUIDE DOG

I'M CLASSIFIED AS AN ESSENTIAL WORKER

Essential Hospital Workers

You might be surprised, but there are a lot of people that make a hospital run beside doctors and nurses. There are receptionists that book patients in when they arrive at the hospital.

Busy porters are responsible for the transfer of patients from one part of the hospital to another. If you fall and break a bone, radiographers are still needed to take x-rays. Millions of women get pregnant in the US each year. All these women need ultrasonographers to scan their bellies!

Physiotherapists are essential to help people get back on their feet after a bad illness and build up strength in their muscles again. Believe it or not, these are only a handful of the jobs involved in the running of a hospital!

Food, Glorious Food!

If supermarkets were closed people would eventually run out of food and go hungry. There are many more jobs involved in the running of a supermarket than meets the eye. Of course, there are the checkout workers and those that help stock the shelves through the night. Have you thought about how the food arrives at the supermarket? There are thousands of truck drivers who go up and down the country dropping off food to the supermarkets from the factories that produce them.

Other essential workers include fire fighters, police officers, journalists, pharmacists, postal workers and government workers. There are thousands of essential workers needed to keep a country going.

No More Vacation... For Now

Did you know that millions of people travel by airplane every day in the US? That's a whopping number of people traveling for work and for their holidays! Flying has become common and has made the world a smaller place.

Coronavirus spread rapidly across the world because of air travel. People infected with the virus unwittingly carried it to other countries. Most experts agreed on this, and, therefore, travelling was limited in an effort to curb the spread of the virus. In previous pandemics this wasn't as big an issue as people didn't travel as much as they do today.

Of course, stopping travel was never a long-term solution to the problem. People need to travel for work, and many people have family members living in different parts of the world.

As the numbers of coronavirus infection went down, people were gradually allowed to travel again. However, this had to be done cautiously. Experts continue to keep a close eye on the numbers of coronavirus infections coming in from people travelling from other countries.

Airports across the world now check your temperature to make sure you aren't showing signs of infection. This can help control infected people travelling to other countries and spreading coronavirus. Many experts also advise masks to be worn when flying. People with fever, cough or any other suspected coronavirus symptoms are not allowed to fly (until they have recovered).

Quarantine (kwor-in-teen)

Quarantine is one way people can still go on their vacations and not spread the virus. Many countries have decided when flights arrive at their airports, every person on the flight will need to be put into isolation for 14 days. This is called quarantine.

Passengers leaving the airport are told to strictly stay in one place and not to meet others for at least two weeks. If by any chance they are infected with coronavirus, they will have very little contact with anyone and therefore will not be able to spread the virus.

However, there are so many potential problems with this. For example, how would they go out to get food? If they are on vacation, they may not know anyone who can bring them their necessities. Some countries have decided they will have a special place for people to quarantine. This may be a hotel or other place providing accommodation specifically for this reason. Hotel staff will check temperatures on a daily basis to see if anyone develops a fever or any other symptoms.

In fact, some airlines are not letting people fly until they have got a special certificate by a doctor. This means to go abroad, you would need to see a doctor first, to ensure you have no symptoms of the coronavirus. The doctor would then provide you with a certificate confirming you are well, and only then can you fly.

All of these measures may seem a little formal at first glance. However, they are all important in reducing the likelihood of full lockdowns in the future.

The idea is that if everyone continues to do things cautiously, then some normality can be retained!

EXTRA FACTS FOR BRAINIACS

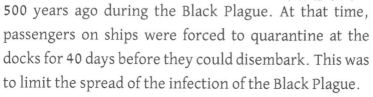

Did you know that quarantine is not a new concept? It comes from the word quarantena which was used around 500 years ago during the Black Plague. At that time, passengers on ships were forced to quarantine at the docks for 40 days before they could disembark. This was to limit the spread of the infection of the Black Plague.

PPE: Personal Protective Equipment

Have you heard the term PPE before? It is equipment to protect you at work.

PPE is used in many jobs and includes helmets, high visibility clothing, ear plugs, safety footwear amongst many other types. An astronaut's space suit is a type of PPE! There are lots of different levels of PPE. It needs to be up to the task. What protective equipment you use will depend on what your job is and how likely you are to come to danger.

Every job has its own risk. A fireman needs to be protected from…fire! They wear fireproof overalls. Construction workers are at risk of heavy objects falling on their head, so they wear safety helmets. If they are cutting wood or metal, they need goggles to protect their eyes. Airport ground staff work near loud planes all day, so they wear noise-cancelling earmuffs (also perfect for taking naps at school). Did you know that people who work with x-rays wear lead aprons so they don't go home radioactive? *

*Technically, they don't become radioactive from x-rays. However, the x-rays can cause radiation damage.

In this same way, doctors and nurses have to use specific PPE to protect against the dangers of coronavirus. In fact, all essential workers should be protected while at work. It is the same as they would use to protect against any serious infectious disease. (Infectious just means highly contagious, so it can pass very quickly from one person to another.)

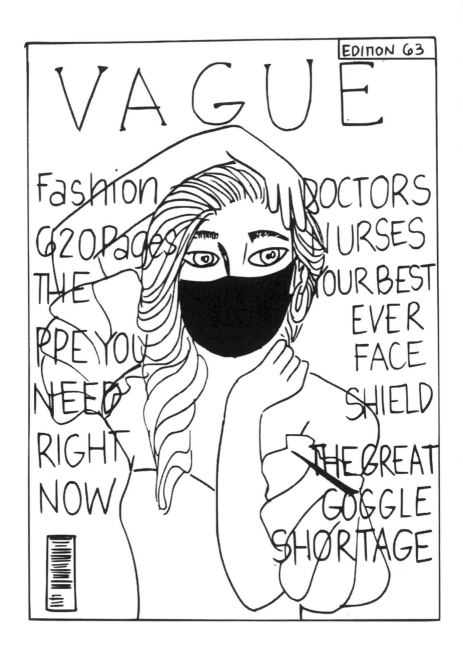

PERSONAL PROTECTIVE EQUIPMENT
FOR HEALTH STAFF
HANDLING CORONAVIRUS PATIENTS

Full protective gear given to staff carrying
out procedures likely to generate
airborne droplets from mouth, throat, or lungs

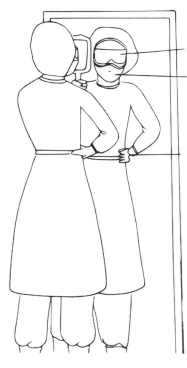

EYE PROTECTION - Full
face visor or goggles

RESPIRATOR-STYLE
FACE MASK

Hands washed thoroughly
before putting on gloves -
pulled over gown sleeve

Health care staff likely
to come into contact with
coronavirus patients but
not carrying out invasive
procedures will be given
gloves, apron, surgical mask,
and possibly goggles

Shortage of PPE

So, where does all this PPE come from? It gets made in factories all around the world. When coronavirus started spreading around the world, suddenly everybody needed PPE, and the factories couldn't make enough to meet demand. This resulted in a big shortage.

You might have seen posts like this on social media.

DOCTOR From the slopes straight to the hospital! # PPE # staysafe # coronavirus # wearingskigogglesasppe # lockdown

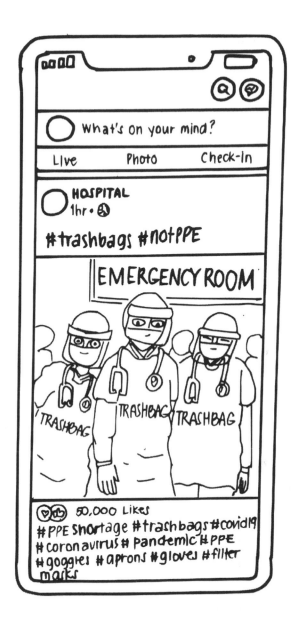

It might seem funny using trash bags or ski goggles as protective equipment, but this actually happened! Hospital workers ran out of protective gowns and visors while treating sick patients with coronavirus and had to improvise!

If You've Had Coronavirus, Can You Get it Again?

Wouldn't it be useful to know if you've already had the coronavirus? Scientists think that if you have had the virus, then it is likely that you will be safe from getting it again for some time. This is called immunity (im-myoon-ity). No one really knows how long you will be immune for. Doctors think that it may be around a year. (This means if someone gets the coronavirus, it is likely that they cannot catch it again for at least a year). Nobody really knows, immunity to the virus could be much longer, maybe even lifelong. Immunity will come up again in the vaccines section.

Testing

How do you know if someone is infected with the coronavirus? After all, the symptoms are often very similar to the common cold.

You have to get a test to find out. There are two types of tests that are available. There is a swab test and a blood test. The swab test is done on people that think they have the virus. The blood test is to check which people have already had the virus and recovered. (Confused? Don't worry! Most Disgusting Doctors get confused by this, too. Keep reading and it will all make sense!)

Swab Test

A swab test is done on people who think they currently have the infection. They may have symptoms themselves or they may have a family member who has the coronavirus.

A swab is just a Q-Tip (cotton bud), the same kind you use to clean your ears, except much longer. First the swab is inserted into your mouth and swished around the back of your throat. The swab then goes up your nose. It feels like someone is tickling your brain through your nostrils. However, it only lasts a few seconds, so it's not too bad. It's a good thing they don't do it the other way around otherwise you might get boogers in your mouth!

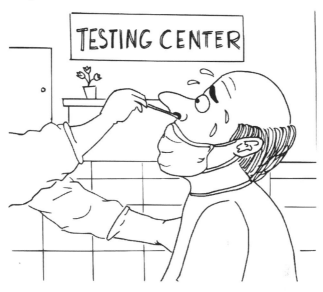

The swab is then sent in a special tube to a laboratory. Scientists examine it using special chemicals to look for the coronavirus. If they find the coronavirus, this is called a positive result. This means the person is infected with coronavirus.

These are real problems hospital coordinators had to contend with. It was a very tricky situation with no right or wrong answer. Different hospitals dealt with it in different ways. Some cleverly used social media to raise awareness. This meant they were able to drum up support in the community. People pulled together and started making masks and gowns at home. The local factories also pitched in and started producing visors using their 3D printers. (3D printers are amazing! They can literally print objects made out of plastic.)

SORRY, THE MASKS AND GOGGLES HAVEN'T ARRIVED YET!

SWAB TEST RESULTS

	PERSON IS INFECTED WITH CORONAVIRUS	PERSON IS NOT INFECTED WITH CORONAVIRUS
POSITIVE	✓	
NEGATIVE		✓

Did you know that most countries have set up coronavirus testing drive-throughs? (Yes, that's right, just like McDonalds but no Happy Meals!) People who are worried they have the infection, can book online and drive to the testing center. They will be asked to roll down their windows and the swab will be done while they sit in the car. This keeps the healthcare worker safe, as they are not spending a lot of time with people that might be infected with coronavirus. It is also much faster for people to get tested in this way.

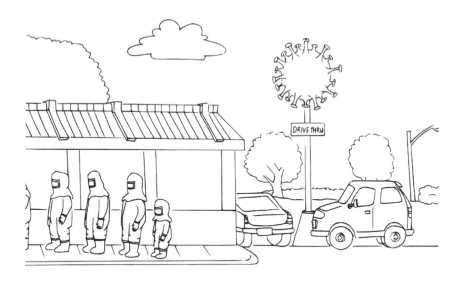

Fake News

There is a myth going around about how to test yourself to see if you have coronavirus. Some say if you can hold your breath for 20 seconds without coughing or your chest feeling tight, then this proves your lungs are working properly. If you pass this test (and do not struggle) according to this, you do not have coronavirus. This is touted as an alternative to a swab test!

All doctors and scientists agree this is FAKE NEWS. If you think you have coronavirus, then you should be speaking to a doctor about getting a proper test.

Did You Know:

What's faster and cuter than the coronavirus swab test?

This might seem like a random question. The answer is dogs! In England, six adorable dogs are being trained to sniff out coronavirus. Dogs have a very keen sense of smell and are able to pick up subtle scents from those infected with the virus. All it takes is a half second sniff. They are highly accurate, too. Nine out of ten times they get it right! This is a much faster and more pleasant way to detect coronavirus infection. Don't be surprised to find these furry healthcare workers in an airport or train station near you.

Blood Test

If you think that you have already had the coronavirus and gotten better, you might choose to have the antibody blood test (the word antibody will make more sense after the vaccines chapter). This is not as bad as it sounds. A small drop of blood is taken from your fingertip using a tiny needle. The blood is dropped onto the test and it reacts with chemicals.

The test will be positive if the person has had coronavirus and recovered. The test is positive when a line at "T" appears. (You can ignore the line at "C."

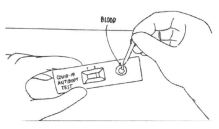

BLOOD TEST RESULTS

POSITIVE	COVID-19 Antibody Test	Positive means the person has PREVIOUSLY had the coronavirus
NEGATIVE	COVID-19 Antibody Test	Negative means the person has NOT had the coronavirus.

This stands for "Control" and lets doctors know that the test is still working properly.) Remember, this does not mean that the person has coronavirus just now. It means they have already had it.

LEADERSHIP

You already know that most people who become infected with coronavirus will not have any symptoms. So, if you were the leader of your country, how would you know what proportion of the population have been exposed to the virus? This is why many countries are doing mass testing. This means carrying out as many tests as possible. By doing mass testing, they can build up a picture of where the infection has spread. For those in charge, this is very useful information. This can help decide where and how to give resources. For example, in areas where there are high numbers of infection, more PPE will be needed.

U.S.A

AREA WITH LOTS OF POSITIVE RESULTS. SEND MORE PPE!

Contact Tracing

If you are only going to remember one thing, this should be it. Contract tracing is really important, and every expert agrees all around the world that it is the best way to crush coronavirus!

Contact tracing sounds complicated, but it's really not. Almost every country that has had an outbreak of coronavirus now has a team set up. What does this team do? When a person tests positive for coronavirus, the team's job is to phone them straight away. They ask the infected person to list exactly where they have been and who they have spent time with over the last couple of weeks. We know coronavirus is highly contagious so it is important to find out who this person may have spread it to.

The job of the contract tracing team is to get in touch with all those people. The team informs them that they may be at risk and need a coronavirus test. Wow, that seems like a ton of tests! The truth is, it is! A lot of countries do not have enough

tests for this. In reality most of these people will be told to self-isolate instead.

How does this help? By asking those people to stay at home for two weeks, it ensures they cannot spread the virus further.

EXTRA FACTS FOR BRAINIACS

Contact tracing has been used for centuries to control viral outbreaks. Viruses spread through a chain from one group of people to another. When you are able to identify the spreaders, and the people who are at risk, you can break this chain. This is a tried-and-tested, low-tech method. You don't need a lot of expensive tests. You don't need any special equipment. Just a group of willing volunteers (the contact tracing team), a phone and maybe a clipboard!

Contact Tracing App

As great as the contact tracing team is, there are some difficult issues to contend with. Picture this: your neighbor tests positive for the coronavirus. The contact tracing team phones her. She tells them she took a bus to the grocery store. How would the contact tracing team get in touch with everyone that was on that bus? After all, everyone on the bus is at risk and needs to either be tested or told to self-isolate. But the problem remains, how would the team even work out who was on this bus?

Wouldn't it be great if there was an app that could do all of this? After all, there is an app for everything! You can order an Uber or pizza through your phone at almost any time of the day.

Well, good news! App developers have been working hard on a contact tracing app. It has been trialed in various countries already.

How does it work, you might wonder? Most phones have a special feature called Bluetooth. When it is turned on, it allows other phones to connect to your phone. When someone tests positive for the virus, they can update the app. The app then contacts all other phones that have been within close vicinity to this phone recently. It informs those people that they have been close to a person who has tested positive for coronavirus. These people can then be tested. If testing is not available, they can self-isolate.

Think of the app as a robot version of the contact tracing team that lives on your phone.

Back to the example of your neighbor. She would upload her positive coronavirus results on the app. The app would then notify all those that were on the bus at the same time as her. Quite nifty, isn't it?

This way, the app has done most of the work for the contact tracing team. Voila!

LEADERSHIP

How does this all sound to you? A phone app that knows where you go, who you spend time with and even knows your medical test results? You might be concerned. Don't worry, lots of people are troubled by this. Could this be an invasion of your privacy? Very good question! Each person, before downloading the app, needs to make their own mind up about how they feel.

The good news is, the app information is all anonymous and private. This means that although people will be informed that they were near someone with a positive result, the app won't actually give their name.

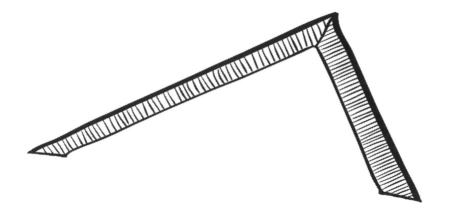

SECTION 4:

The Race to Find a Cure

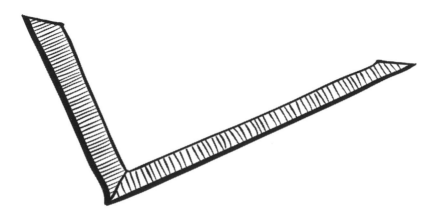

Is There a Cure for the Coronavirus?

Covid-19, the disease caused by coronavirus, is new. It is important to remember that even brainiac doctors are still learning about it. Scientists make new discoveries almost every week. The good news is that most people won't need any treatment at all. They will either be asymptomatic or may just have mild symptoms.

I Tested Positive but I Feel Fine

Most young people and children are likely to be in this category. How many people do you think have no symptoms at all? You might be surprised that so far, all the research done tells us that it is about half. That's right, half the people with coronavirus won't even know they have it! These people will not need any treatment, but remember they can still spread it.

This Feels Like Last Year's Cold

Mild symptoms of coronavirus are usually cough and fever. The treatment is the same as any other viral illness. Doctors give medication to settle the temperature down and usually advise lots of water, juice and plenty of rest.

Someone Call 911. I Don't Feel So Good!

Some people will need to go to hospital. Usually it is because they are struggling with their breathing. Doctors think this is due to inflammation inside the lung tubes. This means less oxygen gets from the air into the blood. These poor souls may need to spend a few nights in hospital getting oxygen through a mask. Once their oxygen levels are back to normal, they can usually go home to rest and recover.

Critical Care

Very, very few people (note the two verys) will need more help than just oxygen. If they continue to struggle with their breathing, they may be moved to the critical care unit (sometimes called intensive care) in the hospital. This is where they might need the assistance of a ventilator. A ventilator is a special machine that helps them breathe.

Critical care is a specialized unit for very sick patients. It is likely you won't ever have been in one of these! If you have, you will know, there are very few beds but a lot more nurses and doctors. There is usually one nurse looking after each patient.

This means the patients can get a lot more attention and are very closely monitored. After all, they are the sickest patients in the hospital.

Sadly, some of these people will not survive. Coronavirus can be serious for a small number of people and this is why doctors and scientists are working round the clock to help find a cure. Everyone, including you, needs to work together in a concerted effort to help crush the coronavirus.

EXTRA FACTS FOR BRAINIACS
Valuable Ventilators

A ventilator is a machine used commonly in critical care units in hospitals. A ventilator is often a last resort to help the sickest patients with breathing problems. When a patient is very unwell their body can get so exhausted that it is an effort for them to breath. Doctors can then connect them to ventilators.

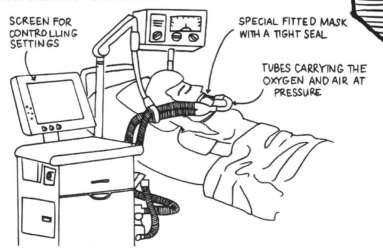

SCREEN FOR CONTROLLING SETTINGS

SPECIAL FITTED MASK WITH A TIGHT SEAL

TUBES CARRYING THE OXYGEN AND AIR AT PRESSURE

The ventilator cleverly pushes air and oxygen into the patient's lungs. Essentially, it takes over their breathing for them and prevents their lungs from collapsing, ensuring fresh oxygen continues to flow through their body and increases their chances of recovery.

Medication

Since the coronavirus pandemic began, experts have been looking for a medication that could cure the illness. The annoying thing is, that because the coronavirus is new, no medication exists for it already. Disgusting Doctors and brainiac scientists got to work. They have been carefully examining every drop of gruesome fluid they can extract from patients to see if they can find answers!

Doctors started looking for a cure by trying out medications that are already used for other diseases. Often the same medication can be used to treat lots of different types of illnesses.

So far, only one medication has been shown to be effective in helping with coronavirus. This medication reduces the inflammation and can help people recover easier. The great thing is that this medication is already widely available around the world and even better, it's cheap!

It is called dexamethasone (dex-a-meth-a-zone) Please DO NOT try and get your grubby hands on this! A doctor needs to prescribe it for you, if they feel you need it.

Sadly, despite all the efforts of nurses, doctors and hospital staff, they are not always able to save every life. Unfortunately, some people who contract coronavirus will die. Many people around the world have already died from this horrible disease.

EXTRA FACTS FOR BRAINIACS

Before the coronavirus, most countries had enough ventilators for the sickest patients. However, the coronavirus created a lot more sick patients! Critical care units filled up quickly and there was a sudden shortage of ventilators.

Where do you think ventilators come from? If you were in charge of making sure hospitals did not run out of ventilators, what would you do?

Well, they get made in different factories around the world. You could order more from the factories that make them. The problem with this is that every hospital around the world had the same idea. They all needed ventilators! The factories that make them sold out very quickly and couldn't produce new ones fast enough.

What else could be done?

Did you know that presidents and prime ministers of countries around the world have powers which allow them to ask big factories to change what they are producing? They can be told to build ventilators instead of what they normally build. These powers are usually reserved for times of crisis, like war or pandemics. During the coronavirus pandemic, GM Motors stopped making cars and switched their production to make ventilators instead.

Other companies like Dyson (yes, the vacuum cleaner) also lent a helping hand. They developed a ventilator for the National Health Service in the United Kingdom.

Pop-Up Hospitals

You've probably heard of pop-up burger joints. But have you heard of a pop-up hospital?

Coronavirus caused a sudden surge of new patients for hospitals. There were lots of people arriving at hospitals with symptoms of coronavirus. The hospitals filled up quickly and the beds ran out! To accommodate for this, many countries around the world started building makeshift or pop-up hospitals. Different countries took different approaches, but the principles were the same.

In New York, a field hospital in Central Park was built. They had tents set up with beds, ventilators and doctors ready to accept patients. In the United Kingdom, they turned massive exhibition halls into hospitals to keep up with demand. In China, workers built a new hospital from scratch in 10 days!

Vaccines

The most high-tech gadget you own is not your smartphone or even your Nintendo Switch. It's your body! The human body has built in antivirus "software," and just like your phone, occasionally you need an upgrade. Vaccines are that upgrade.

Before you can understand how vaccines work you need to learn a little about the ingenious immune system. Your immune system is what fights off infection when you become unwell. When a baby is born, they have no immunity. Newborn babies have never been infected by any viruses before and so have no way to defend against them. That's why toddlers often catch one virus after another.

When a person becomes infected with a virus, their immune system kicks into action. What does this mean? We have red and white blood cells. The red cells are what make your blood red and they carry the oxygen all around the body. The white cells are the body's defenses. They are like soldiers at war against a virus invader. As soon as the white cells detect a foreign virus, they start producing weapons to attack it. These weapons are called antibodies. Once the virus is destroyed, the antibodies are stored away in case this same virus returns.

These antibodies cannot be used as weapons against other viruses. Each virus will need its own antibodies to fight it.

- **This is not strictly true. There is some transferred immunity from the mum through breast milk and through the placenta.**

Before vaccines, the only way your immune system could learn to protect you from a virus was by getting infected in the first place. That's far from ideal.

This is where vaccines come in!

Edward Jenner invented the first vaccine over 200 years ago. He was a Disgusting Doctor from England. He would take scrapings from the udders of infected cows and rub them on the arms of small children! Completely gross! He figured out that by taking smallpox scrapings from cows, he could trick the children's white cells into producing antibodies for smallpox without them getting infected.

Many vaccines are still made based on these principles today. Don't worry, no one's going to be rubbing any udder juices on you! Thankfully, scientists have found a way to do this in a cleaner way in labs. A vaccine is made by taking a live virus and using special chemicals to deactivate it. This deactivated concoction is then made into a vaccine, and doctors give it commonly as a shot.

When you get the vaccine your white cells recognize this new dead virus. Then they start producing the antibodies required to fight it. You do not become unwell, as the virus is deactivated. Simple and very clever, right? If you do eventually get exposed to the actual virus, your body is in a great position (with antibodies at the ready) to fight it off immediately.

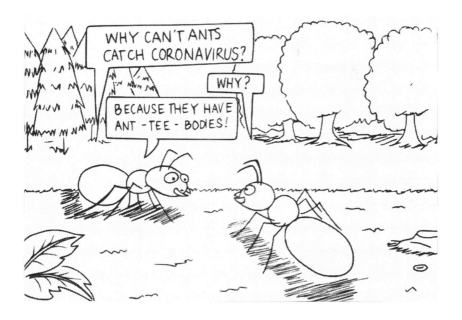

Not All Antibodies Are Built the Same

Antibodies are like specialized weapons. They need to be made custom and unique for each type of infection. Usually an antibody for one virus will be useless against a different type of virus.

Most people around the world have had the measles shot, so they will have antibodies in their blood against measles. These antibodies will not work against coronavirus infection.

Did You Know:

Alpacas are awesome! They look like llamas but are usually a little smaller. Three alpacas called Big Boy, Emperor and Blue Eyes have been gaining fame around the world. Scientists predict they could be key in the fight against coronavirus. They have discovered that when alpacas are exposed to the coronavirus, they produce tiny antibodies. These antibodies are smaller and actually better at getting into pockets of the virus and attacking it. It is hoped that one day these tiny antibodies can be isolated and used as treatment in humans against coronavirus.

We're taking the bus?

Alpaca my mask

Victorious Vaccines

Since vaccines were invented, they have saved countless lives. Lots of infections that used to kill people hundreds of years ago, are now very rare. Some have even disappeared completely.

Did you know smallpox killed an estimated 300 million people in the 20th century? It was last recorded in 1977 and thanks to vaccines has never infected anyone since then!

Remember the Blood Test for the Coronavirus?

This test is used to check if someone has had the coronavirus. If a person has had the virus, their white cells would have already produced the antibody weapons. The blood test detects these antibodies. This is why it is called the antibody blood test and it only works on people that have already been infected.

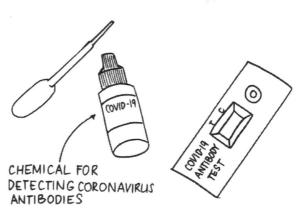

CHEMICAL FOR DETECTING CORONAVIRUS ANTIBODIES

Coronavirus Vaccine

Vaccine production is known to take a notoriously long time, often 10 years or more! At the time of writing this book, lots of organizations around the world are busy working on a coronavirus vaccine. Some are using the more traditional method of a deactivated virus in a vaccine. Others are trialing newer techniques, using RNA and DNA. This is all disgustingly interesting, but we won't go into that just now.

You wouldn't think so, but making the vaccine is actually the easy bit! The tricky part is testing the vaccine in order to make sure it is safe to give to everyone. This is called a trial.

Scientists take a potential vaccine and first test it on animals in labs. If it is found to be safe and showing promising results, then it can move onto the next stage. It is tested on small groups of human volunteers. These people are monitored very closely for months. Doctors check to see that the vaccine is working and make sure it has no side effects. The whole process can take years! If all goes well over time, it will be deemed safe.

Most countries have a committee made up of doctors and scientists who will examine the results of all these trials. Only when they are satisfied that the vaccine is safe will they allow the general public to receive it.

The good news is that there are lots of coronavirus vaccines that have been made. A few of these are already in the process of trials!

Once deemed safe, the vaccine can be manufactured in large quantities. It will then be the job of those in charge to ensure that as many people as possible get the vaccine. This will be a worldwide effort. It will be the single, most effective way to crush the coronavirus!

EXTRA FACTS FOR BRAINIACS

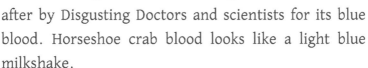

Did you know that horseshoe crabs are essential to finding a coronavirus vaccine? This gruesome crab is sought after by Disgusting Doctors and scientists for its blue blood. Horseshoe crab blood looks like a light blue milkshake.

Its blood is special because it can recognize harmful toxins very quickly. Scientists take this blood and mix it with batches of vaccines. This is how they check if the vaccines have any toxins. If there are any toxins in the vaccine, the blue crab blood will quickly clump together and become solid. The crab blood is essential to check that the vaccine is safe enough to be injected into humans.

A Peek into the Future: Telemedicine

Since the coronavirus pandemic began, doctors have had to adapt how they see patients. A doctor's waiting room and office can be a hotbed for infection. The last thing you want is to catch coronavirus from your doctor! With many states in the US under stay-at-home orders, patients were advised to avoid visits as much as possible. Telemedicine was the solution.

Doctors around the world have been embracing this new technology. Patients no longer have to go into the doctor's office and can instead have a virtual visit from home, using their phone or laptop. In fact, telemedicine has become so high tech that doctors can now examine patients over the video call.

Many use a digital stethoscope to listen to patients' heart and lung sounds. Once they have completed their examination, the doctor can email prescriptions directly to the drug store.

Telemedicine has grown remarkably around the world. It is impossible to predict what the world will look like after the pandemic. What is clearer is that telemedicine has made it easy, convenient and safe to see your doctor. In the future, it is thought that up to 30% of doctor visits will be virtual!

Did Anything Good Come from Coronavirus?

The coronavirus pandemic has caused increased stress in most people in one way or another. Everyone has had to adapt to the new normal of social distancing, wearing masks and working from home. There have, however, been some positive outcomes, too.

With more people staying at home and less cars on the road, there are a lot less pollutants. NASA has reported a massive reduction in air pollution in big cities around the world. In fact, skies have become so clear that people in the Punjab in northern India reported seeing the Himalayan mountains for the first time! Doctors in China have estimated that due to this cleaner air, many thousands of children and elderly people's lives have been saved.

Disgusting Doctors Bowing Out

Well done, you've reached the end of the book!

Thank you for taking this Disgusting Doctor journey in learning more about the coronavirus.

The year 2020 has bonded the doctors and scientists of the world closer together. Working on treatments and a vaccine has been a worldwide effort. To try and curb the spread of the virus, compromises and sacrifices have had to be made by everyone. Now that you know more about the coronavirus you can play your part, too!

Have fun spreading your knowledge and dispelling some of those pesky myths. Remember, new information is coming out all the time and you can visit cdc.gov for the latest.

One final piece of good news: scientists predict we are not far from an effective vaccine!

Fingers crossed for summer vacations next year!

About the Authors

Dr S G Jack is the penname for Dr Saira Goheer and Dr Jack Miftha, who wrote the book together. They are both doctors and also happen to be married! No easy task writing a book together.

When Dr Saira is not seeing patients, she likes to bake cakes for birthdays and weddings. She has an avid fascination for creating things out of buttercream and refuses to work with fondant! She has an insatiable sweet tooth and tells her patients, "Do as I say, not as I do." Her favorite mode of transport is an electric scooter.

Dr Jack loves all things tech. He spent most of his childhood breaking things apart and putting them back together again. He has an obsession with space and loves nothing more than to argue with moon-landing deniers. When he isn't seeing patients, he likes to cycle, cook or play Playstation online with his other doctor friends. He isn't very good at Call of Duty.

More from
Disgusting Doctors

If you enjoyed this book, we think
you will love our next one too!

We have included the introduction
for a sneak peak. Enjoy!

If you would like to order the book
please visit
www.disgustingdoctors.com

TEN TERRIBLE IDEAS DOCTORS USED TO THINK WERE WONDERFUL

• Disgusting Doctors •

Dr. S G Jack illustrated by Ana

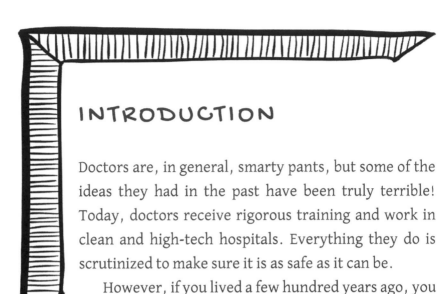

INTRODUCTION

Doctors are, in general, smarty pants, but some of the ideas they had in the past have been truly terrible! Today, doctors receive rigorous training and work in clean and high-tech hospitals. Everything they do is scrutinized to make sure it is as safe as it can be.

However, if you lived a few hundred years ago, you weren't so lucky! The hospitals of the past were dark, dingy and unsanitary places. Most wealthy people preferred to get their medical care at home. Only the poor who couldn't afford this went to the hospitals as a last resort. Treatments were often experimental, based on hearsay and myths.

One of the most terrible ideas of the past were barbers moonlighting as surgeons. That's right, barbers performed operations in between cutting hair! Going to your barber to get your leg amputated may seem peculiar now. However, this was the norm for thousands of years! These barber-surgeons never attended medical school and instead learned through years of practice and a little bit of guesswork!

Shockingly, operations were carried out without wearing masks or gloves. In fact, surgeons didn't even wash their hands before cutting a patient open and fiddling with their guts! What's even crazier is that watching surgery was considered a form of entertainment. It was entirely normal to catch up with your friends at the operating theatre. A lovely evening of sharing snacks and watching a random stranger have their gallbladder removed!

To this day, the rooms in the hospital where surgery is performed is called an operating theater. Although don't try and sneak in to watch!

Did you know about these terrible ideas?

Doctors use to "treat" a head injury by drilling a hole in the skull!

Doctors use to "cure" arthritis by advising their patients to sit inside a rotting whale carcass!

Doctors use to "test" for diabetes by tasting their patient's pee! Revolting!

This book delves into the gory history of doctors from the past and some of the more bizarre ideas they have had. Keep reading if you want to find out why Egyptian mummies were crushed up for medicine, or why people in England used to drink human blood to help cure their ailments!

Be warned, some of these chapters will make your stomach turn!

Thanks for reading!

If you would like to order the book please visit www.disgustingdoctors.com

Made in the USA
Middletown, DE
16 October 2020